Bull Hill Fest

By Cameron Macintosh

Bull Hill Fest is on today!

Fliss has a hat stall
at Bull Hill Fest.

Nat has a roll stall.

I am hungry,
so we call at Nat's stall.

Max sells his crops
at a stall.

We get a bunch of big figs
and small plums.

We get some plum jam from Max, too.

You pull up the top to get the jam.

Joss has a drink stall.

Mum got me a tall drink.

I am full!

Nick has an egg stall.

At his stall,
Jess can pat Nick's best hen.

Jeff sells plants at his stall.

Dad gets a plant to put on the wall in the hall.

We all had a ball

at Bull Hill Fest!

CHECKING FOR MEANING

1. What does Max sell at his stall? *(Literal)*
2. What can you get at Joss's stall? *(Literal)*
3. Why was there a hen at Nick's stall? *(Inferential)*

EXTENDING VOCABULARY

stall	What are the sounds in the word *stall*? What does *stall* mean in the text? What other sorts of stalls might be at Bull Hill Fest?
roll	What shapes can bread rolls be? What is another meaning of the word *roll*?
full	What are the sounds in the word *full*? What word means the opposite of *full*?

MOVING BEYOND THE TEXT

1. Bull Hill Fest happens in autumn. What is autumn like where you live?
2. Which stall would you most like to visit at Bull Hill Fest? Why?
3. There are figs and plums at Bull Hill Fest. Have you ever tried figs or plums? What is your favourite fruit?
4. What is winter like where you live? If Bull Hill Fest happened in winter, how would it be different? What kinds of things might be sold at the stalls?

SPEED SOUNDS

PRACTICE WORDS

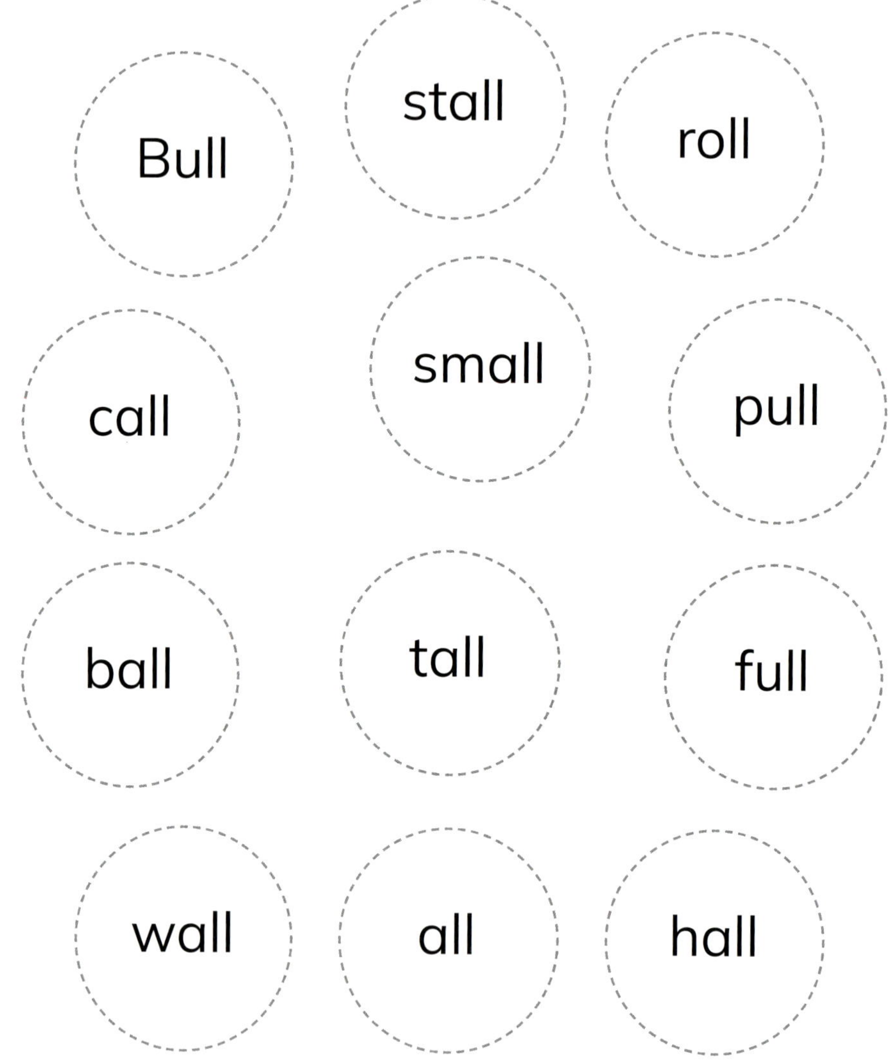